LIGHTHOUSE

KAI WRIGHT

Revolving Door Press
CHICAGO, IL

Cover art by MuddaGoose
Author photo by Kikomo.P Imagery

ISBN 978-0-9990148-3-7. Copyright © 2017 by Kai Wright. Published by Revolving Door Press, Chicago, IL. All Rights Reserved. Manufactured in the United States of America.

contents

The Social

Creature   11

Holster   14

The Love

What Key Largo Makes You Think About Home   17

Hello.   18

For the Boy Who Would Not Let Me Love Him   19

Untitled. II   20

Bear.   21

The Self

Faith Without Works   25

The Smoke Poem   26

Nothing To Me   27

Faith Pt. II   29

Untitled. I   30

Faith Pt. III   31

introduction

When I first saw Kai perform the poem "Creature" at the Chicago Teen Lit Festival in 2016, I was in awe; the depth of subject matter, the sophisticated play with language, and the unforgettable imagery were, I believed, beyond the capabilities of such a young person. I was so glad to be wrong.

Kai has a fearlessness in her work that most writers—or people, for that matter—don't possess. In the aforementioned poem, the speaker explores what it means to be a young Black man in America. Kai writes: "Creature cry and they call him feather / tell him he can't float / that he needs to be tree / stuck in one place, only to uproot him." Black masculinity is unreasonably defined by many contradictory interpretations born from the white gaze.

The short collection elegantly vacillates between despair and hope, however. Though there is violence, there is also beauty. Kai explores, for instance, the ways in which the female body is subjugated while still acknowledging the strength of womanhood. In the poem titled "Faith Without Works," she writes:

"I praise her in the most mundane ways / Fearing nothing / As I crawl into her belly / She's the beast I pray to every night." There is a definite celebration of the self in the midst of these tumultuous and oppressive times.

Kai is a poet we should be watching. Her writing holds so much promise. With skillful allusions to contemporary poets, it's a work that pays homage to it's predecessors while uniquely engaging with the world around her.

I'm honored to introduce Lighthouse.

— Erika L. Sánchez, 2017

This book of poems is dedicated to Alyssa Travis. You were a major inspiration over the course of writing this book, and your friendship gave me the confidence to reach into parts of myself I otherwise wouldn't have. Without you I don't know where I would be. Thank you for everything.
I love you.

The Social

Creature

In the midst of history a decision was made
to create a being so powerful it wasn't
even God-fearing
because it looked to much like him.
It stands proudly in the face of the sun
because it isn't afraid to burn.

This is for the creatures who talk slick under they tongue
who make drums strong with hearts that beat polyrhythms in they sleep.
Creature has gunshots for lullabies.

Creature be trapped in his own skin.
Creature be boxed in, creature be wind in a box.
Creature be Terrance
Creature be magic
Creature be mensa

—told to conform
as they turn Creature dirt
turn Creature scum, twisting under boot
turn Creature spit festering in the back of your throat
coming to a boiling point trying to teapot its way out.
Creature be running like the wind
with nowhere to go.
His life be treadmill with false horizons.
They telling him he can catch up.
Creature be left with little to no oxygen and told to breathe.
Creature still running
hoping his feet will turn wings
hoping he can outfly his destiny.

Creature be lucky to so see 20.
Creature be Tamir
Creature be Keith
Creature be Cameron

When Creature bleed they call it rain

spoon feeding him lies until he believes them
telling him he's made out of broken glass
fallen from class project houses
telling Creature he conjured up concoctions
swallowing mediocrity until he's made of it.
Creature mind is labyrinth.
Creature body is ink when headlines read:
Creature Body Sprawled at the Corner of Statistic and He Had It Coming.
Nobody gives a damn.

Creature cry and they call him feather
tell him he can't float
that he needs to be tree
stuck in one place, only to uproot him
prying at his pride
ripping away his childhood.
Creature never known childhood.
Creature came out the womb with a target on his back.
Creature be black as silhouette plastered at the back of a gun range.

Some say Creature ain't got no substance.
Creature ain't got no choice.
They yelling dead or in jail.
Nigga, pick one. Pick now.
Creature be Jason
Creature be Edwin
Creature be Kj

I say Creature be gold
but some still say Creature be game, creature need to be tamed
so hunter take Creature crown
gun take Creature crown
cuz searing bullet be the only thing hot enough to pierce gold
strong enough to break through Creature breastbone
that doesn't even fear God
or fear himself.
Creature be Laquan

Creature be Freddie
Creature be Eric

This is for Creatures whose lineages don't start where they are
Creatures that are taught that they were created to be convicts.
Creatures be crabs in a barrel.
Creatures be lions in a cage.
Creatures be wind in a box.

Creature spirit cannot be tamed.
Creature be wading in the water cuz he can't swim,
but he can jump
and he can fly.

Creature still running
the horizon his finish line.

Holster

If we are all made in his image

I hope he doesn't wear a uniform and a badge.

The Love

What Key Largo Makes You Think About Home

once I watched the sky and it reminded me of you.
the clouds in combat
triumphantly marching their way into battles, sewn
into a tapestry of sunrises.

a northern breeze twisted and turned them into men,
and like men do,

                              in the shadow of a morning sun,
on a day as calm as this one,

they brawl to the death.

I wondered   how could something be so beautiful and so violent?

I already knew the answer was you.

Hello.

I wanted to tell the world I loved you before I wanted to tell

you

        had given me an envelope with my name on it.

this

was second grade all over again.

        only this time I was invited in.

now you're inviting me into your life.

    I tell your mother what a lovely home
        she has made for me inside of you,

there to bring me comfort food and condoms

if need be.

you said ...

        means the same

as I love you.

        I wonder if it hurts the same, too.

For the Boy Who Would Not Let Me Love Him

more often than not

you close the door before you invite me inside

more often than most

you ask me how I'm doing and then tell me that I am not wanted

why do you leave me questioning the feeling in my stomach

I play with voodoo and Venus to make you see that I am not the woman who made you think you were of this world

flesh and debris

I have done more to crack open my sternum
and build a home for you
than she ever will

but you keep closing doors.

Untitled II

Sometimes I wish I was more easily silenced.
I think I'd find comfort in the arms of men
who would bare me if I did not speak.

I bet men would fall at my feet,
throwing their falsely advertised loyalty to me
if I turned a blind eye and sat,
offered myself wholly to the command of anything—
surrendered.

Gilded in affirmation and brawn.

I'd like to be blissfully ignorant,
painlessly in love,
broke-backed into a bitch and house-trained
to piss on cotton when you are too lazy to take me outside,

offer myself wholly to be commanded into anything.

Bear.

He is papa bear.
I am cub.

He is shallow.
I am warm.

He is caught.
I am tainted.

He is weight.
I soar.

The Self

Faith Without Works

Without living inside the 27 walls of my home,

without peeling back layers of sheetrock to find a girl horizontal,

you couldn't tell me what it means to hold on.

Have faith

and float in a forever.

You could never know God quite as well as I do.

I hear her sermons with my feet,
sing hymns that ripple like bath water lined with lavender, swallowing
rain,
petroleum,
acetone,
and my self image.

I praise her in the most mundane ways,
fearing nothing
as I crawl into her belly.
She's the beast I pray to every night.

The Smoke Poem

One night, you decided you
would wear my scalp as a wig.

My teeth, pendants
and my spine, your cane.

You had me wrapped
around my finger,

carved your initials into my back
and I cringed at their sight.
I told you

to infiltrate my body,
pour out my comfort and replace it with you
so I would never forget what fear leaves in my hips.
Make my skin home,
fall over me like a cloak,
fondle the folds of my brain
harvesting memories for your taking.
My thoughts are no longer mine

because they all went up in smoke.

Nothing To Me

There is nothing to me but lines.
I am pencil
underscore
hair follicle at the roof
of your mouth where your tongue can't reach
a nuisance.
I am punctuation,

the end of a sentence

but I am no question mark.
Nothing on my body curves
leaving men searching for answers
wondering what's behind my margins.
I am crease in notebook pages,
unnatural enough to agitate, but not enough for you to care.
I am smoldering embers left from an addiction to burning paper.
Lung disease.
I am not affluent
not fluid
abundant in edges
and corners.
I am empty FedEx box with a label that reads return to sender.
I am smoke detector and fire alarm
sharp
piercing
like the dilation of pupils.
Picture frame,
door frame.
I am not scissors.
I do not cut on purpose
just by happenstance
as you happen to be standing on a Lego.
I am Lego
small but deadly enough
to shift your weight from my edges.

I am often asked why I don't bend
snap
crack
asked why I choose to be solid
and not melt into a mold you created.

Faith Pt. II

Peel back the wall and find a girl sitting in her bed with her knees bent.
I pat her on her shoulder.
I know the type of sadness that longing brings.
She feels unworthy.
I tell her it's easier to let go.
I have done my work.

Untitled. I

When rain falls
no one cares to listen.
Confusing the pounding of heart with the soft caress of water on glass
or pavement
or skin
Disregarding the warmth water gives.
No one wants to hear God cry.
No one wants to feel relief.

Faith Pt. III

                         Sometimes I don't like preaching.

Sometimes I don't like being the savior
      or being God's only daughter
that no one seems to mention.

Forced to watch men pass me by then look to me for answers,
ask my mother for guidance and try to profess that I am of flesh.

                         How many books have you read
                         that tell you I'm not jesus?
                         What voices do you hear
                         that claim I'm not the most high?

How can I not be when I've been singing all my life,
wading in water
swallowing my pain
oiling my body
purifying the names of men
baring their lies
harboring truth
sanctifying and crucifying my womb
rolling up pages of a holy book
mapping the stars
bleeding out
crying out
making homes out of stories
making Heaven on Earth
running
dancing
laughing

      Tell me:
is this not the ultimate sacrifice?

acknowledgements

I would like to thank you, Kevin Rogers, for being a painting I could never fully understand. You will always be art to me.

bio

Kai Wright is 16-years-old and a junior at Jones College Prep in Chicago, IL. She started writing when she was 6, but started writing poetry in 7th grade. She is a member of the YOUmedia Louder Than A Bomb youth slam team. Poetry has become her saving grace.

about revolving door

Revolving Door Arts is a nonprofit organization and press committed to empowering creative community and evolving the artistic craft of new, young, and emerging writers and artists. Revolving Door Press publishes works by teen and adult writers to further elevate the voices and stories of and beyond our time.

teen chapbook series

2017

The Bare Backside, Semira Truth Garrett

Northwest Ordinance, Jalen Kobayashi

Brown Visitor, Nyvia Taylor

thank you

We would like to thank our Board of Directors, Advisory Board, the Chicago Awesome Foundation, our partnering writers and authors, all of our generous donors and others who have made the Revolving Press Teen Chapbook Series a success.